Inspired

How to Motivate Yourself into Creating Something Great

HENRY WOLFE

INTRODUCTION

How do you go from being broke to becoming a millionaire? If you have a job, it will be hard to break your regular routine and do something different. A job is a place where you work on someone else's vision to earn money for yourself while furthering their agenda. While working on a job you should always learn and build your skills NOT to stay, but to build something for yourself and your family. Think of it this way; if you or someone in your family becomes ill are you able to take and extended amount of time off? When you return to work will management have a problem with you taking the time?

The majority of jobs have a set amount of time that you can take and depending on the circumstance there is FMLA, but if you earn paid time off, once it is gone there is nothing to cover you financially. Time off with no pay results in financial hardship. Bills and responsibilities steady pile up. We all want to be secure so we are able to be there for our loved ones, but jobs do not provide that level of security.

Don't get me wrong. If you are on a job and you love it and your desire is to climb the corporate ladder and save your money that is great and I wish you the best. There is nothing wrong with that. However, I hope this book opens your mind to different ways of thinking and will make you desire more. If you are already a builder with your own vision and want to make your own way and leave a legacy for your family, then you are well are your way. Get ready to be inspired!

TABLE OF CONTENTS

1

WHY IS IT IMPORTANT TO BE YOUR OWN BOSS?

A good swift kick in the butt is necessary at times. Open your eyes and realize that you are put on this earth to be great! There is no reason to lead a mediocre life when you have the ability to be exceptional! You can do better and you know you can. Today decide that you will no longer sit back and wait for something to happen and you will not make excuses for why it cannot happen. You are a go-getter and YOU make things happen. It is time to go to your next level!

Being your own boss means you make the decisions and you decide what type of money you will make, what hours you will work and how far you will go to make it a success. You are only as good as your product or your plan. When you have your own business you have security knowing that no one can fire you or make you feel bad for not meeting THEIR standards. You set the bar and you reach it!

In order to do anything you need money to start and to hold you over to be able to pay your bills until your business starts to make a profit. Do not quit your job to start a business or quit too soon after beginning. As you progress you will know when the time is right to work your vision full time.

I want you start small and do something that brings in an extra hundred dollars a week.

What idea do you have to bring in extra income? When I was in college I sold T-Shirts. I found companies to get quality shirts and a print company that did good work for an affordable price. I sold shirts for five to ten dollars each. It made the extra money I needed, but I was young and did not stick with it. My advice to you is if you find something that is making money... stick with it!

Once you have decided what you want to do go ahead and get started! Increase your income by another hundred each week. Do not spend the money that you are making, but reinvest it into your business. You are doing this little exercise to see how viable your business or idea is to your customer base. Once you have worked your idea for thirty days if you do not make the extra hundred a week then maybe you need to consider something else. I recommend thirty days because everything takes time. In this stage you have to have a lot of ideas because the first one hundred may not work. I'm not saying it's going to take a hundred tries before you find the one that works for you, but it might. You have to be persistent in whatever you do. Giving up is easy, but staying in it for the long run will pay off in the end.

Other than selling T-shirts I had started about thirty-five businesses before I found one that worked. I had businesses that made money and I had businesses that ended up costing more than I got out of it. I kept on trying because I knew that it would work out one day. Getting started is the easy part, yet being consistent and seeing it through to the end is hard. If it does not work the first time keep trying. No matter what you decide to do you have to work it to ensure that it will be successful.

Once you get that first sale or deal done you have the blue print. Keep using it to get what you want. Becoming a millionaire is hard work, but you can do it! No one is going to hand it to you. You have to earn it! If it wasn't hard work then everyone would be a millionaire. I always tell my children a man that does not work does not eat. Well in business... a man that does not try is not successful.

Think about all the things that move you. Do you have a hobby? Do your parents have a business? I am telling you to sit and brainstorm. What can you do? You cannot depend on a job. When the owner decides to sell or close the company what will you do? Take control over your life and depend on you. Make sure that you take care of you. Who could care more about you than you?

Nothing in life is guaranteed except what you put your force and effort to. That is the only way to make it happen. If you are fresh out of college or an older worker with that threat looming over your head that one day you may be out of a job; make your security guaranteed.

Most families want their children to go to college and get a great education. That is awesome, but why not have a place where they can use their education and have a guaranteed position. We all want to be able to leave our children an inheritance and make sure everything is taken care of. This is the way. If you don't do it for yourself, then think about your children and your family. Working on a job is not going to get you there. It is important to be your own boss to get security for your family. Take back the control you have given these companies. Secure your future.

The time you spend making someone else rich can never be regained. Those minutes, hours, days and years that you have given to make it happen for someone else could have been spent securing your future and creating stability and wealth for your family. Your children, family and friends need you to spend time with them and create memorable experiences, however, if you are on a job you are not going to be able to do that.

You are always at the mercy of someone else. You have to get up early to go to work. Your children get themselves ready for school and when they get home from school you are still at work. By the time you get home you are tired and trying to wind down. That means there is less time that you are spending with your family. The average person works Monday thru Friday just trying to get to the weekend. On the weekends you are tired and want to sleep in to catch up on your rest. Decide today to take control of your life and secure your future and the future of those you love.

HENRY WOLFE

2

GETTING STARTED

———————•◦•———————

What can you do right now to start generating revenue for your business? What are the things that move you? What do you want to try? Do you want to be a baker? Do you like fixing bikes? What is it that gets your mind going? What are you good at? My advice about starting your business is to figure out what you can do right now that will bring in money. Starting a business is about generating that first flow of cash to see if it can work. Don't focus on the passion and all of that stuff you have heard over the years. When you are starting your own business you need to focus on the current cash flow. Is this idea making me money and can I save enough of this cash to invest it in a bigger idea?

When you start out testing ideas you are doing your market research. If you created or bought a shirt and people are buying it then you know that is a good item. If you have a shirt and you only sold one in the last month then that shirt is not a good item and you need to discontinue it. You don't need to say "hey, I can buy these cheaper", so you invest your money in an item that does not sell. What is going to happen is you are going to have a lot of that item, it will not sell and you will be out of the money you spent. Your money will be tied up in that product and you will eventually lose out from bad practices.

When I started my T-shirt Company I

went into a discount store and I saw they were selling T-Shirts with prints on them that I liked. I realized that they were priced at three dollars each and I thought to myself "can I buy these shirts and resell then at a greater price?" I took sixty-five dollars and bought twenty shirts. I increased the price to six dollars each. Yes, I doubled the price on a shirt that I bought out of a discount store.

I started selling the shirts everywhere I went and to everyone I knew. I think I sold out of the first group of shirts in two days. I went back and got forty shirts and I sold out in another two days. When I went back to the store they were out of shirts, so I found another store and bought more T-Shirts I liked.

I repeated the process, but after a while the stores stopped carrying the shirts at the price I wanted them. I didn't get down and say "well I can't sell shirts anymore because the store is out". I found a local T-shirt company that sold shirts in bulk and I went and bought five cases of shirts in all different colors and went to a website called Alibaba. I contacted several companies in China and asked them to send me samples of their prints and in about a week I got all kinds of free prints and samples to use. Eventually, I wanted to use my own designs on shirts and I sent them to the company to create.

Even though it was more work having to go through the process of buying bulk shirts and taking time to create prints I stuck with it. I did not get stuck in the box with my thinking and I did not give up! I wanted to keep my cost at three dollars per shirt, so I made sure that my shirts did not cost more than two dollars and each print was not costing me more than fifty cents. This did not feel like work because I was enjoying myself, learning something new and if felt good to be able to make my own money.

I contacted local stores and they agreed

to sell my shirts in their stores. I had expanded past selling shirts to those I knew and on the street. My business was growing. I believed that I could get my shirts into larger retail stores, but they had minimum order requirements and they wanted me to reduce the price of my shirts, so they could make a substantial profit.

I went back and forth trying to negotiate, but it was like talking to deaf ears and the stores didn't hear me. I was unable to move forward with the larger stores. I am not telling you this to discourage you, but I want you to learn from my experience.

I stopped selling shirts because I could not get them into bigger stores. I should have kept doing it the way that made me money, but instead I gave up because of a small defeat. Do not let this happen to you. If one company tells you no; keep doing what you are doing the way you have been doing it. DO NOT STOP! You never know where your business may take you in the future and sometimes we are so consumed with what is happening that we forget that we are still doing well, our business is still successful and we are GREAT!

3

DON'T BELIEVE THE HYPE

ome people give horrible advice. I have asked people how I figure out what type of business I want to open and the advice I have gotten was to do what I love and could do for free. That is hyperbole and it is just plain hype! Who wants to work on a job and their boss comes and says "Do you love your job?" And when you say "yes" your boss responds by saying "Great! You can do it for free!" It is not practical or realistic to give your time to a cause or a product and don't receive any compensation for that effort. The same should be when you are in business for yourself. Don't do anything without the intention of getting paid.

The truth is that even if you are doing what you love, it will take money to pay your bills and to get your supplies in order to get from point A to point B. I understand that people mean well when they say do what you love, but the more realistic option is to do what makes you money and then when you have enough money... do what you love!

In the bible, the book of Matthew twenty-four...it talks about talents. God gave three men talents and two of them used what they had to increase in knowledge and skill. In other words they used what they had to gain more. There was one man who buried his talent in the ground. In the end when God came back to see what they did with what they had. The guy that did not use his talent was scolded because of it and his talent was taken. This parable shows me that we are supposed to use our time, efforts and money wisely. What we have been given to do and work with we need to use it to multiply or gain more, so that we will be secure. Your business can't grow without money and you cannot pay bills with love.

My thoughts are to do what makes money and if you love it then that is a bonus! I love real estate. I love everything about it from learning about houses, apartments and even learning about land. When I became a real estate agent I worked twelve hours a day. I went into the office at eight in the morning and I didn't leave until eight in the evening. Needless to say I was the first person in the office and I was the last person to leave the office. The funny thing was even though I loved real estate I was not making money as a real estate agent. No matter how hard I tried I did not make one sale. I could not sell a piece of property if it fell in my lap. I was spending my money trying to make this thing work. I was advertising, I was walking thru neighborhoods putting flyers in mailboxes. I even mailed over ten thousand letters and post cards to everyone in the city. Nothing happened for me.

After seven months of not making any money I had to go get a job at a grocery store stocking. It did not pay much and even after I got the job I was still going into the office in the evenings and working as an agent. I really wanted it to work. The passion was there I loved real estate, but it did not pay the bills.

I was married and with three children and not having and income was a strain. My wife carried the bills for a few months and even though she never voiced it, I know it was a strain. This is the point in my life when I realized that working on something you love does not necessarily mean that you will eventually be able to live off of it.

The reason why doing what you love even if you do it for free does not work is because money takes care of things NOT passion and NOT love. Love is just a feel good emotion that can't get you anywhere in business. Love will lead you down the wrong road in most cases. Think to yourself of how many stupid things you did for love. Love is good, but do not let it cloud your decisions when it comes to business and stability. If you love it and it only brings you pain then you need to give it up and focus your mind an energy towards something else. I loved real estate, so that is what I thought was going to get me to my destiny, but what got me there was me being practical

That brings me a back to the top of my story. I got a job at grocery store to pay bills and my wife was pregnant with our fourth child and I know I had to do something and it could not be emotional; it had to be practical. I thought long and hard about what I could do to start a business and make money from the second I started doing it.

After a while of brain storming I moved from a grocery store to a restaurant that paid more and they did not limit my hours. I was able to get overtime. Things were great at first. There was more money, more hours and there were chances to move into a management position. The problem with that is after a few months management changed, my hours decreased along with my checks. I continued to work there, but I never stopped thinking about practical business ideas.

Little by little I saved money and began looking for businesses to buy. I thought about buying a sub shop and was pretty close to doing so. I made contacts with the owners and made an offer that they accepted. I had an attorney draw up the contracts and revise the contracts several times so that the deal would go through. After a while of going back and forth and bunch of money being spent on attorney's fee the deal fell through. I was crushed! I did not give up on the idea of being self-employed. Not matter how discouraging the journey became. I just changed my plan.

I paid bills as usual and since I thought that I was buying the sub shop I quit my job thinking that everything would go through (which is why I told you not to quit your job too soon). At this point I had to do something quick. The first thing that popped in my mind was to drive cab. My father was a cab driver and I knew the business from him even though I had never driven a cab myself. I took my last twenty-five hundred dollars that I had in savings and bought a 2000 Ford Windstar van for five hundred and twenty-five dollars. I used the rest of the money to paint the vehicle the company colors of red and white, do the lettering on the sides of the cab and do repairs on the van to make it run smoothly. I got my chauffeur's license and business paperwork and went to work.

The first day and night I drove my cab I made four hundred and twenty-five dollars and from that day I knew that anybody that wanted a business had to be practical and not emotional. In the first two weeks I made my initial investment back and the rest was profit. I felt like I finally got a break through and things were starting to work out. I was not doing what I loved, but I began to love what I did because it was making money.

I started to understand the principle of practicality. This is a principle that I created to help people understand what the meaning of life or business should be. As far as business, the principle relates like this; whatever is practical in your life is where you should start. Your father or mother may not have been in business, but you have to take what you know and put it to use. Whatever you learned as a child or even as an adult you have to use it. Be practical and not emotional.

4

DOMINATE

————————•◉•————————

You go into business to dominate. Business is not for the person that just wants to say I have a business. Business ownership is definitely not about bragging rights. Being an entrepreneur is hard work. The reason why so many people have jobs is because they want to be comfortable. Think about it. People stay in dead end jobs because it is their familiar. They know what to expect when they go to work, how much money they will get paid each week and they are comfortable with that. They don't want to have to push themselves on a daily basis to figure out where their next pay day is coming from.

When business is slow at my company there are times I find myself going on and on about how to increase my business revenue. My wife always tells me to be grateful because on a slow day I can make what the average person makes the entire week. I am thankful, but I do not base my success off of the income of other people or off of their decisions regarding what is enough for them. I base it off of what I am trying to achieve.

I am always thinking of ways to expand and increase revenue. If other people are satisfied in taking a whole week to make four hundred dollars then that is on them. If they are content then that is fine and I am not judging them for what they are satisfied with. I personally am not content with that and I keep pushing myself to grow beyond what I can see or think.

Education is great. It is always a good idea to be educated on things, but wealth cannot be gained by education alone. Education does not guarantee a great job. Education does not guarantee more pay. It does guarantee in most cases a large amount of debt.

Think about all the billionaires who started out going to college, but dropped out. Bill Gates and Mark Zuckerberg are college drop outs. Zuckerberg became a billionaire five years after he dropped out.

There are many people who have degrees and do not even work in the field that they are educated in and they work in places that do not pay them what they are worth. I have no problem with being a college graduate and I am not speaking badly about it. I have a degree in business myself, but I just wished I had known more before I got myself into all this student loan debt.

What I will say is you have to be willing to learn something new every day to dominate whatever space you are in. When I get up in the morning I say to myself I am going to make one million dollars to day. In my head, heart and soul I believe that I am going to make a million. I also know that this might be the day I create a million dollar product to bring to market. It's crazy... I know a guy that when he talks about business he always says "I have an idea, but I don't want to tell you because I don't want you to steal my idea." I always tell him that I might be the guy that helps you bring your idea to market. I may know someone that can help you push this from idea to actual product. I feel he just doesn't want to break out and be a success and he will never dominate until he can change his mindset.

Mindset is everything when you are in business. You have to know that you are going to do whatever it takes to make the venture work. If that means putting in extra hours, losing sleep or whatever is needed you are willing to do it. You have to see yourself a success. You have to speak that you are a success. Vision boards are great tools to make sure that you stay on track. When things come up you have to REFUSE to be defeated. Do not waste your precious time making excuses of why you cannot get started and when you do start do make excuses for why you cannot finish.

You have to constantly grow whether it is your mind, business or family. You have to keep your business growing. Without growth your business will die. Think of when a flower grows and reaches its maximum height and destiny. You will get that fresh fragrance and nice beautiful flower, but it dies because it has reached its' potential. This is what happens to a business when you get comfortable. Once you set a goal and reach it you will not go any further unless you create a new goal. You will shut your doors and close for good because things are always changing and you have to have the ability to think ahead.

Business in my opinion is a lot like marriage or any valuable relationship. You have to put forth the effort to grow and to try new things. You need to produce new ideas, memories and now new times. You have to add new love every day. Don't allow your business to stop because you got comfortable. You have to live your life looking forward and stop looking at what you had before. What is in the past is in the past and you cannot move forward looking backward. You have to approach business with the mindset of what value can I create today that I have not already created. I encourage you to learn something new every day. Even if it just helps you shave five minutes off of a process that is growth. How I grow in my business is if I see that I am not growing I look at other businesses and I learn from their success.

When I see they have a successful idea or plan I tweak what they have, so it will fit my business.

About a year ago, when I was buying cars and business slowed down I went from buying a hundred cars a month to only four a month. I said to myself if I don't snap out of this my business will die! You may say well that was only a month where things got bad. The problem is when you let your mind get comfortable in mediocrity your business will get that way. You will say it is the economy, the location, or even the customers. Whatever makes you feel better and gives you a reason not to strive for better. In my business I don't have time for excuses it is either do or die. Anybody can come in my business and dominate. I look at everyone as competition or the person that is trying to push me out of my space.

When I get up every day I remind myself that I must DOMINATE. I have to be the best car buying business in the city and the competition is heavy. There is a junk yard on every corner and there are car buyers on every corner. What I did since I did not have the capital like other companies is dominate. I had to reach every customer before those bigger companies. I had to be nicer, negotiate harder and move faster if I want to take over my industry. I just don't say that I am going to make a million dollars. I say I am going to change my sector of the business into a multi-billion dollar business.

5

DRIVEN TO SUCCEED

Y ou have to be driven to succeed in order to dominate. You need more passion and more desire than another company, store or associate out here. When you decide what you want to do and how you want to do it and you go after it with a vengeance. When you choose to start your company people will tell you that you are a fool...that your idea will never work. They will even tell you don't waste your time because your venture is not going to be successful.

They are going to try and get you to stay in the same rut that they are in or give you their ideas on what you should do. People who don't live on purpose don't really want to see other people succeed. They want you to fail, so they can say "I told you so".

The people that you expect to encourage you the most will most likely become the most distracting people you will encounter and they will be an enemy of your vision. I have experienced first-hand where family tried to sway me from what I knew I wanted to do. They encouraged me to get a good job and save money for a rainy day. The problem with that idea is that I could not settle for my fate being in the hands of company. I was a little perplexed by the actions of those close to me because I felt that they were supposed to believe in me, help me and keep me on the right path. If I did not have the will power to keep saying no and fighting for my vision I would be on a job that I hate making less then

I should be making.

As a child my mother worked two jobs cleaning houses. She took classes and became a nurse. Nursing provided for us, but just because she was a nurse did not mean that we live the good life. My father was there, but he had many issues that I will not discuss and he rarely helped with the bills. To make a long story short we were barely able to make ends meet. I have seen how hard it is to work hard and give a job your all, but still are not able to live the good life. I saw how my mom worked and I knew that when I was old enough and able I would want to be my own boss.

There have been plenty of times when my close family have told me that I am crazy for desiring to live in the more expensive neighborhoods or even thinking about being rich. I have actually had them to get angry with me and call me stupid, tell me I dream too big, I don't live in reality, etc.... We have too many people telling us that we cannot do it because we are not smart enough, tall enough, skinny enough and the list goes on and on. You have to be driven in your thinking and mindset to get past all of the negativity. I really feel when you are starting out you should never tell anyone the direction you are going in. If you want to start something new I would say just do it. You are going to be very excited about your idea and plan. You will want to share it with everyone, but do not take a chance on a family member or friend injecting negativity into what you want to do. It will cause you to doubt the strength of your idea.

If you are working on a job right now that is fine. I have worked plenty of jobs. I just knew that a job was not my ending and it should not be yours. It doesn't matter where you start it just matters where you finish. You can work and have money, but you should always have a bigger goal. Always look forward to financial freedom.

6

IF THE CHICKEN DIDN'T HATCH, DON'T COUNT IT!

I am a guy that believes that you are supposed to think forward and I always know what I want before I go out. However, there is one thing that I have learned over the years of running my business and that is to never count my chickens before they hatch. Back in the earlier days when most families were farmers and they depended on their livestock to survive they had to know exactly how many animals they would have to provide for, so they would go out and count up all of the fertilized eggs of the chickens to estimate how much chicken scratch to buy. In life nothing is guaranteed except change, so they may have set in their minds that they were going to have a thousand chicks, but there is no way to make certain of it.

A predator may come in and eat half of the eggs, a storm could come and wipe them out, the eggs could crack, etc... So many things could happen to stop this farmer from collecting all of his chicks. This is the same for business. It is good to make goals and look forward to profit, but don't spend according to what you will make, but according to what you have in hand. What I am saying is don't think of the sale as done until it is closed and you have gotten the check deposited in your bank account.

In real estate for instance, you may feel that you have this deal done. Your customers loved the house, the offer got accepted, and the home inspection looks good and then the bad news. On closing day you get that call that something has happened with financing and you aren't going to be able to close. How many times has something like this happened; where you felt that the deal was done a BAM something stopped it and it did not happen?

You could have done everything by the book, but because of the mere fact that you were depending on that commission look what happened. Always make sure that you go above and beyond to make sure everything is done whether you and your client is supposed to do it or not. What happens is when you leave the work that should and is supposed to be done by the other side it does not get finished? Go above and beyond to make sure for you and your clients sake that everything is done. You cannot stop until you have the check deposited into your bank account and you can see the total on your billing statement.

On one occasion I had two clients that were great people. They were buying land in the area they told me they wanted over two acres, high land and a corner lot preferably. I took them out and they found the lot they loved and it was a cash deal. They offered cash and it was accepted. The problem is the other agent and his client were supposed to provide the survey of the property and a perk test for the land. They were also going to pay for the survey and the test to be done. The problem was after I spoke with the agent and his client they were like they were getting it done as soon as possible. Three weeks later when we are about to close I called that agent and asked where was the survey and the perk test. He tells me we thought that you guys were getting that done. I then asked him how did he think we were getting it done and his client was supposed to pay for it. After another week his client sent the check and I was able to set up the survey and the perk test and have that done. Three weeks later we got the results that the land was buildable and we could close. We set a closing date one month later. If the other agent and I were on our a game we would have caught this mistake and had it taken care of, but because we left it for the other one to do it there was delay in getting it done. I could also say that it was the other agents fault, but I could have called to check up on the progress. Since I made that mistake learned from it and now make sure to cover all my bases for every deal.

7

EXPECT MORE!

E xpect more out of yourself than you ever thought was possible. If you think that you could have a million dollars think and believe that you can have a hundred million dollars. On my social media page I tell people to stop thinking about being a millionaire and start thinking about being a billionaire. We have become accustomed to asking God or the universe for just enough to pay our bills and to make ends meet. What if we started asking and believing for more than just enough?

I say start asking God for the world and see how much of it you can get. When I speak about asking God for these things I am not talking about sitting in a room and just asking him to give you the world without putting forth any action. You must put some action behind your thought and while you are working towards your goals you are putting out the positivity into the atmosphere.

The aurora around your life wants to see how big you can think. The same effort that you use to ask for just enough you can use that same energy and ask for abundance. I am a prime example of how I asked for more and got it. I speak all the time that I have a million dollars in my pocket. I say this because I believe it and I know that it is there. Whether it has manifested or not I can say with confidence that I have a million dollars.

If you own a business I am certain that you did not start it on the basis that you are just going to make enough and you barely want to make it. You go into business to make millions and you believe it is going to happen. The only reason you stop believing it is because you experienced a failure or the people around you made you feel that it would not work.

In life you have to work more when you expect more. If you want to lay around on the couch, eating chips and watching TV you will not get more out of life all you will get is less life and more fat on your body. Every day you have to push yourself until you can't go anymore.

On a job if you go earlier and stay later your boss will take notice and with that hard work you will get more pay and a better life. If you make excuses about why you can't go work earlier and why you don't want to work harder you will keep getting what everybody else is getting.

When I was a Welder and I went to the

boss and asked for more hours he asked how many hours can you work over-time I said I can work as many as he could give me. That is when I was sixteen and I was working ninety hours a week and I was bringing home a thousand dollars a week. My mother came to pick me up from work and asked if she could open my check. I said sure and I still remember the comment that she made. She said "Wow you make more money that your dad!" I was not better than my father. I just worked hard and was not afraid to ask for more.

8

BOOT STRAP

———————•❖•———————

Stop thinking that there are investors out there to come put a pile of cash in your hand for your great business idea. They are not out there and if you do luck up and find one that is willing to listen they probably will not invest in your business. It is hard to understand, but the truth is most people are looking to get rich quick. Yes even rich people are looking to get rich even quicker. From my experience I have talked to several millionaires and they don't want to hear a story of a guy who is working hard with a regular idea that is going to make a good return on their money. They are looking for you to come to them with an idea that you know will never have a chance of being successful. Most rich people that have money to invest don't want regular returns like ten to twenty percent return. They want your idea to be a Facebook idea that will make them billions. Just like in life those ideas aren't around for everyone to have them. My advice to you is start small and work and save and bust your butt to get to the next level. When you save an extra thousand dollars, invest that back into your business. Every time you have excess capital invest it in more product and or equipment. I have told you I have started several businesses and while they were unique I had no big investors lining up to give me their cash. I started these businesses with the cash I had in my pocket. I started at the bottom and learned how to make money. I also learned that if I did not manage my money right I would lose it all and have to start over again starting from nothing. Do not bother investors because you are wasting your time. I would recommend that when you start your business you use every waking hour to pour into your business. Use every dime of profit you make put it into inventory and keep doubling it. And let's say after ten to twenty years of grinding it out you won't need investors because you will have several million dollars in the bank. If your product is that great someone will approach you to buy it from you. Time is over of people thinking that this great person is going to come pour hundreds of thousands of dollars in your business because you make great cupcakes. That just doesn't happen and I am the person to be real with you and tell you that.

HENRY WOLFE

9

GET OFF YOUR BUTT AND BE GREAT!

t took me a long time to open up my mind and know if I wanted to be great and make a difference that I would have to get off my butt. I am not talking business wise I am talking heath wise. I have struggled with being overweight most of my life. As a child when I was in high school my weight ballooned to 265 pounds. I was able to lose 90 pounds and maintain a healthy weight. There was a

55

time span where I was a healthy weight of 175 pounds for about seven or eight years, but once I got married my weight ballooned to 375 pounds. I hate to say this, but when I started my cab business I worked long hours and thought more about making the money then being healthy. However, today is a different day. I am here now to inspire you to pay attention to your health and the health of your family.

Health is important because if you are not healthy then how can you enjoy the benefits of all of your hard work. I can also say that I am now paying attention to my health. I have gotten off my butt and ramped up my health quest. I have lost 20+ pounds to date and I am more amped about my life than I have been in a long time. I go to the gym two sometimes three times a day and I feel good about it. I know that I am seeing the results of my hard work. I am not listening to anything negative that is going to get me off of my quest.

What I found out about inspiration is once you start doing it and you share it, other people will be drawn to what you are doing if they need to get healthy. If they need to change bad habits in their life because you are a positive force that will move people to follow what you are doing. Don't be discouraged because after they get what they need they may fall from your circle. You can't let that stop you, all you have to know is your actions got them to think differently and that made a difference in their life.

Now that I am going to the gym I can see a difference in my wife's eyes. She is even going to the gym with me to get toned up because she said that she wants to make a change in her body. Even though I do not think she needs it that is where my positive action creates another positive reaction.

Think back to a time you did something positive for yourself, family, friends and strangers. You created another positive action in the universe and that set off a great shifting of the minds of your circle and the circles of those people around you. This type of thinking changes more than just your thoughts and dreams, but it transcends generations. Everyone can benefit from positive thinking and living a fulfilling life. If you never thought that you can impact the world I dare you to do something positive and expect positive change from that action. You are great and the world is a great place to be! Get off your butt and be Great!!! Be Inspired to do something different and Inspire others to do the same and we all can make this world a better place.

16024404R00032

Printed in Great Britain
by Amazon